Spirituality

UNDERSTANDING IT
AND PURSUING IT

Spirituality

UNDERSTANDING IT
AND PURSUING IT

Peter Dennis

CAPCO
International

Spirituality: Understanding It and Pursuing It

ISBN: 978-0-9698926-7-0

Cover and text design: WeMakeBooks.ca

Printed in Canada

CAPCO International
7 Ashdown Crescent
Richmond Hill, Ontario
Canada, L4B 1Z8
Telephone: (905) 771-1543
E-mail: peter@peterhdennis.com
Web site: www.peterhdennis.com

This book is also available in electronic form and may be downloaded from most Ebook retailers.

Acknowledgements

Nearly all of the ideas and concepts presented here originated with someone else. Most are either ancient or came from others whom I have been privileged to encounter, either in person, on recordings or in books. Some of these individuals and sources include: Abraham (Esther Hicks), Bashar (Darryl Anka), Herbert Benson, Deepak Chopra, Wayne Dyer, David Hawkins, Napoleon Hill, Barbara Marciniak, Ricardo Martinez, Marcia Moore, Michael Newton, Earl Nightingale, Dr. Peebles (Don and Linda Pendleton), Stephen Pollitt, Seth (Jane Roberts), Dick Sutphen, Michael Talbot, Brian Tracey, The Transeekers (Anne Morse), Neale Donald Walsch, Gary Zukav and the list goes on. To all of those above and to those appearing in the Bibliography, many thanks.

As well, I thank my hypnosis clients, all of whom have contributed to my learning in more ways than they realize.

Finally, without the helpful suggestions and hawk-eyed editing of Carol-Ann Dennis, Kristen Large and Billinda Pita, this manuscript would have been a far lesser document. A special thank you to them.

Introduction

This book was originally intended to be the second edition of my earlier book (2004) on the subject of Metaphysics. Shortly after that book's publication, it became apparent that there aren't many people who understand what that subject is about, or care to pay money to find out.

Meta means beyond and physics refers to the physical. Metaphysics, then, is the branch of philosophy that deals with the non-material or the spiritual.

Through the intervening ten years, it also became apparent that Spirituality is a subject in which many people have an interest. That led me to changing the title and abandoning the idea of creating a second edition of the first book.

Over the past few years, I also came to realize that Spirituality is not so much about what we know as it is about what we do. Considering that, I have eliminated many of the metaphysical concepts from the first book and have concentrated on presenting an understanding of Spirituality and how to advance it. You might find this to be more of a how-to manual than the previous book.

The ideas you will find here could challenge a number of your beliefs and, if that's the case, I ask that you keep your mind open to the possibility that there may be something to them. The bottom line here is: If an idea or an action gives you peace or makes you feel good, you are probably on a track that is right for you. I hope that in reading this book, you finish it feeling better than when you started it.

Table of Contents

PART ONE

Understanding Spirituality

THE CREATOR

There are many ways to approach an understanding of Spirituality, but here, we are going to start at the beginning. Of course, from the big picture perspective, there was no beginning, but from the perspective of human beings, things did have a beginning and this is where we will start.

To understand our beginning, it is important to understand the difference between cognitive knowledge and experiential knowledge. To illustrate, if you were a non-swimmer and wanted to learn to swim, you could read some books on the subject, you could speak with experienced swimmers and you could watch people swimming. All of this would give you some cognitive knowledge of the subject but your understanding would still be incomplete until you jumped into the water and felt the water's buoyancy, pressure, temperature and practiced Newton's third law of physics: For every action, there is an equal and opposite reaction. With this experience of being in the water, your understanding of swimming would become much richer and much more complete.

The Creator (sometimes called God, Source, All That Is, etc.), who had created everything, had a cognitive understanding about all of creation. It did not, however, have the experience of everything, and it realized that, without experiential knowledge, its understanding was not as rich as it could be.

The Creator, then, set out to acquire experiential knowledge of all of creation so that it would have a richer knowledge of everything and so that it would have new things and experiences to create. That's the idea behind how our reality began.

That idea gave birth to The Creator dividing itself, and in a sense, going off in all directions to create experiences for itself. It divided, sub-divided and fragmented to cover all of the dimensions, realities, universes — everything, everyone, everywhere and everywhen. Interestingly, each of these Creator fragments was holographic, meaning each piece had all of the power and information of the whole.

WHERE WE FIT IN

Now, to understand our role in all of this, imagine a few of these all-powerful, holographic Creator fragments floating around in some unimaginable place and debating what they should do to create a new experience for their enrichment. I'm sure they didn't float around in some place or actually debate, but in my limited imagination, I can see that they might have somehow hit upon the idea: "Hey, how about we experience something totally different from what we are? OK, what?"

Well, we are unified (all is one, one is all) so let's experience disunity or separation. Also, we are unlimited, so let's experience what it's like to be limited. Two ideas, totally opposite to what The Creator really is: unified and unlimited.

So, hitting upon that idea, these all-powerful aspects of The Creator set out to create a universe that would provide and support the experience of separation and limitation. They then created time, space, duality and matter, and all of the stuff of what we refer to as our universe.

Next, they had to put themselves into this universe so they could have this experience. They subdivided further down to the level that we call soul. That's where humans come in and it's where we begin to see exactly what we are and what our purpose is.

Specifically, we are those holographic aspects of the Creator. We built this universe so we could have this human experience of separation and limitation. We are The Creator.

As we began our task of creating this universe, we realized that we would have to, in some way, become material or physical. In our natural state, we are not physical; we are made up of the same stuff and have the same power as The Creator because we are The Creator.

The stuff or essence of The Creator is light energy. Our scientists, today, are telling us that everything is composed of energy and so are we. When you are composed entirely of light energy and you want to become physical, you have to dial down the intensity of the energy so that it can support physicality, and this is what we did.

SOULS AND OVERSOULS

To go from our natural level of energy and corresponding level of consciousness (more about this later), The Creator fragmented some unknown number of times until we got down to the level that we call the soul. At the soul level of energy, we were able to animate and sustain a physical body. In effect, we are light energy beings (souls) in a physical body, having a human experience.

The soul actually joins a fetus in the womb to become a human being, and while in the womb is busy wiring the mind of the soul with the brain of the fetus. Michael Newton elaborates on this in his books: *Journey of Souls, Destiny of Souls and Life Between Lives*.

Souls are often referred to as our "Inner-Self". In Metaphysical terms, the Inner-Self is connected to the much more powerful energy known as the Higher-Self or Oversoul. The Oversoul is in charge of many souls and manages all of their human lives, past, present, future and parallel.

Inner-Selves (souls) and Higher-Selves (Oversouls) are pure energy and are not at all physical. Their nature is spiritual. The difference between physicality and Spirituality lies in an understanding of energy.

ENERGY AND VIBRATION

As I said earlier, everything is made up of energy. This isn't apparent to the naked eye but our Particle Physicists tell us that the spaces between the tiniest of sub-atomic particles are vast and are filled with a vibrating energy. These scientists are discovering things that are blowing Newtonian Physics out of the water. For example, the particles they are observing will behave according to the expectations of the observer, something akin to thought moving matter. This study is called Quantum Physics or Quantum Mechanics. The word Quantum is used because the Scientists aren't sure whether they are dealing with a particle or a wave — it varies depending on the observer's expectations.

A feature of this universal vibrating energy is that everything has its own unique rate of vibration or frequency. This applies to humans as well, and this is what is referred to when someone speaks about a person's vibration. This is a common new age term, although, I doubt many people realize that it is something that can be measured by scientific instrumentation. For specific organs, most hospitals are equipped with instruments that can measure the vibration of an organ, such as a heart or brain. For the whole body, it's considerably more complex, it requires complicated engineering and only a small number of such instruments exist. Other ways of getting a handle on human vibration are through applied kinesiology and the use of a pendulum (to be explained later).

Earlier, I said that the energy of a spirit is more intense than the energy of a human. Another way of saying this is that the energy vibration of a spirit is faster or has a higher rate (as measured in hertz) than the vibration of a human.

THE DENSIFICATION OF ENERGY

What I haven't said, so far, is that this vibrating energy can give us the illusion of solidity or physicality.

Just to confuse things further, I also haven't said that vibration correlates with both consciousness (the ability to be aware of oneself and one's surroundings) and density or solidity.

Here's what I mean: A slow vibration gives us the illusion of solidness or more density. For example, a rock has a slow vibration, it appears solid and dense, and it has very limited consciousness — so limited that science can't measure it and doesn't acknowledge its existence, at least to date.

A plant has a higher vibration, less density and a greater amount of consciousness. It can sense where the sun is and lean in that direction, it can sense the location of water and send its roots towards it. An animal has a higher vibration than a plant. It has some non-physical aspects such as emotion, fear, etc. It can also sense danger, care for its young and hunt in packs.

A human has a higher vibration yet. There are mental and emotional facets, which are non-physical, and its consciousness allows it to solve mathematical problems, entertain abstract thoughts and put a man on the moon.

THE SEVEN DENSITIES

If you look at vibrations that are high enough, they no longer give the illusion of solidity or sustain physicality; they exist only in the spirit realm. Some Metaphysicians and New Agers have categorized levels of vibration and refer to them as ranges or categories of density. These densities are also referred to as ranges or dimensions of consciousness.

To illustrate, the common classifications are:

First Density:

- Consciousness is one-dimensional.
- The densest of all physical levels.
- Minerals, elements and compounds exist here.

Second Density:

- Consciousness is two dimensional.
- Carries the frequency of plants and animals.

Third Density:

- Consciousness is three-dimensional and includes the ability to lament the past, worry about the future be aware of the present.
- Humans, dolphins, whales and some primates exist here.

- The Ego is developed here.
- The illusion of separation is strongest here.

Fourth Density:

- This is the last Density for human bodies.
- Individuals here are said to be enlightened.
- Consciousness takes on group identity without any loss of individual identity.
- Time is more malleable, and past, present and future begin to blend.
- The vibrations of negativity are more difficult to maintain.
- The illusion of separation begins to diminish.

Fifth Density:

- This is the First Density of non-physical or Spiritual reality.
- Individuals here are said to have ascended and some are referred to as Ascended Masters.
- Individuals in this Density have an urge to share their knowledge and wisdom with those in the lower Densities. Many become spirit guides.
- Time is no longer a limitation.
- These beings merge with their Higher Selves or Oversouls.

Sixth Density:

- This is the Density of "Christ Consciousness." It is the consciousness of Jesus and Buddha.
- It is the Density of Angels.
- Beings here recall their true identity and see the interest of the whole as completely in accord with the interest of the individual.

Seventh Density:

- Consciousness is multi-dimensional
- This is the frequency where all becomes one consciousness, limitation and separation evaporate, all become one integrated whole again, and presumably, aspects of The Creator get antsy and take off on other adventures.

TO PLAY FAIRLY, WE HAVE TO FORGET

Now, getting back to humans and what we are doing here, there are two important concepts to understand. The first is that, as we are here to have an experience that really explores the concepts of separation and limitation to the fullest, we have to "forget" that we are really unified and unlimited. If we don't do this, we would not be playing the game fairly. For example, how could we fully and completely experience limits when all along, we know that we really don't have any? To achieve this human experience fully, in each lifetime, we are born blanking out or "forgetting" all knowledge of who we are or what we are here to achieve.

THE THIRD DENSITY

The second very important thing to understand is that, although most of us are in the Third Density (3D), this Density is a range of vibration and consciousness that ranges from low vibrating individuals to high vibrating individuals. Those of us at the lower end of the range are living in an environment where most of our lives are fear-driven. We feel disconnected from The Creator and may not even be aware there is a Creator. We feel powerless, unworthy and live with anger, guilt feeling, shame, etc.

Looking at those whose vibration is near the middle of the 3D range, we see more love and less fear. We still see things like discouragement, loneliness and disappointment but there is more awareness that there is a bigger picture and these folks begin to look around with a sense that there is something more than just fighting and surviving.

At the top of the 3D range of vibration, we find the Mother Theresas, Mahatma Gandhis, Albert Einsteins and others who live with much love, acceptance and enjoyment of life. People at this top end of the 3D range are probably carrying a vibration that is approximately a hundred times faster than those at the lower end. For these people, life is good, it's easy and they live with abundance, peace, kindness, gratitude and compassion.

Everyone living in the Third Density is living on Planet Earth and is experiencing the same co-creations as those at the top of the range. The difference is that those with the higher vibrations have an expanded consciousness that allows them to see more of what this reality really has to offer. It's much like everyone is in the same room but those with higher vibrations have more light available to them, allowing them to see more of the room's different features. Those at the lower end, with less light available, are stumbling around, bumping into things, getting beat up, and feeling pain, fear and discouragement.

You could liken the Third Density to grade three in elementary school. The people at the high end of 3D have learned nearly all the lessons that are available from the experiences of grade three and are getting ready to graduate into grade four. People who do graduate from 3D to the Fourth Density (4D) are referred to as "Enlightened". From this term, you might think of it as the lights have come on and they can now see more of the bigger picture or the Divine plan.

Before moving on, I want to point out three further features of our universe that contribute to a full experience of separation and limitation. One is duality. By duality I mean that to fully understand a concept or an experience, it is helpful to experience its opposite. For example, to appreciate hot, it helps to have the experience of cold. Love is better understood if one has experienced loneliness. We understand murder better if we are both the murderer and the victim of murder.

Another important feature of our reality is that we are multi-dimensional. This manifests in two distinct ways: First, most of us live many lives on Planet Earth, in the Third Density. We incarnate numerous times, often spanning thousands of years. We take on different learning missions, requiring different levels of energy, specific genders, body types, IQs, disabilities, etc. — all conceivable variations so as to experience, learn and grow as souls.

Interestingly, from our 3D perspective, we see these lives as existing in the past, present and future. From the higher vibrational perspective of the Higher-Self, where there is no time, they are all seen as happening at once.

Bashar explains this quite well when he uses the example of a film strip. If we let one frame, say somewhere in the middle of the filmstrip, represent our present life, then all of the frames on one side of this frame can represent all of our past lives. Similarly, the frames on the other side can represent all of our future lives.

From the perspective of someone scurrying around in the present life frame, he or she would see the frames to one side as past lives and the frames on the other as future lives. But if there was a projectionist looking down at all of the frames, to him/her, the lifetimes are all happening at once. If you substitute the Higher-Self for the projectionist, you can see how our Higher-Selves can view many lifetimes simultaneously, while we see them as past, present and future.

The second way in which we are multi-dimensional is that each time we come to a decision point in any life, we fragment further to explore all of the alternatives and variations. For example, we may get married to Ralph. If we do, we also don't get married to Ralph, and we do get married to any number of other potential partners.

That may sound pretty bazaar, but if we are here to experience and we are unlimited Creators, why would we limit our experience to only one variation?

A final point before moving on: Have you ever wondered why there are no duplicates? Well, now that you know there is an all-powerful entity setting out to experience everything, do you really think it is necessary to experience anything more than once?

THE SHIFT OF DECEMBER 21, 2012

While there are a number of people on the verge of graduation to the Fourth Density, Planet Earth is making the same transition. Some say that our solar system has recently moved into a portion of our galaxy where the energies are different. It may be surprising to hear this, but Planet Earth is also a conscious entity and it is moving to the Fourth Density as well.

In recent years, there has been a shift in consciousness, in and on the Earth, and on December 21st, 2012, this shifting process took a giant leap forward. Those at the higher end of the third density felt it while those in the lower regions probably didn't notice anything.

If you were able to detect that a shift was going on, you probably noticed that, as a species, we are becoming more civilized — crime statistics and war fatalities are down, and we are engaging in thoughts and behaviours that are more love-based and conducive to raising vibration. Some further signs of this shift are:

Businesses, Boards of Directors, top executives and financial managers are becoming more regulated and transparent.

Individuals, as opposed to a select few, are exercising more control over bank accounts, investments, currency and business decisions. Corporations are exhibiting more social and environmental responsibility. The Internet has contributed much to this, as has social consciousness and social media. Since the crash of 2008, much has shifted.

Education is shifting to more individual-based and creative (right brain) curricula. We see specialized schools for the arts, for athletes and for the trades as opposed to "one size fits all", with the object of teaching conformity, obedience to authority and fear of failure.

Democracy is covering more of the planet. Free elections are being held in third world countries more than ever, and international regulatory bodies and social media have increasing influence around the world.

Religion is shifting to more openness, flexibility and emphasis on community building and good works, as opposed to fear of the Lord, damnation and blind obedience. We have a Pope who is opening discussions that have never been attempted before.

Environmental consciousness has never been greater. Although a good deal of this is the result of fear of such things as rising water, prairies becoming desserts and air being unbreatheable, we are also seeing more responsible management of land, waste disposal, food and water. Examples of such shifting in recent years would be the organic food farms, the growing organic sections in grocery stores and the movement towards cleaner water such as reverse osmosis and distilled water.

We can see shifts in our health care systems. Until recently, all we really had were injury-care and illness-care systems, where only physicians were in charge. Now we are seeing an emphasis on prevention and a movement towards alternative and complementary systems, emphasis on supplements, energy healing, herbal remedies, Nurse Practitioners, Midwives and life style changes.

In communications, we are seeing a shift from the control of a few to more involvement from the everyday citizen. The Internet, social media and freedom to information legislation are all contributory.

THE EGO

Our attachment to the Ego is also shifting as we are beginning to feel our real attachment — to each other and to The Creator (same thing). When we created this Third Density to experience limitation and separation, we felt the separation intensely, and it was painful. With this disconnection, we felt we had lost our true identity, which we had in order to have this human experience. Without an apparent identity, we had an "identity void", and to fill this void, we created the Ego.

Our Ego is a false identity that is standing in while we undergo this experience of separation and its job is to keep our vibration in the 3D range until we have experienced all we can here. As we exhaust the available 3D experiential learning, our Ego dissolves and a sense of our real connection increases. We begin to find that it is no longer necessary to always be right. We don't have to understand everything. We needn't dwell so much on the past and future. Focusing on what's wrong isn't the best way to go. And turning our attention from what's going on around us to what's going on inside of us can be considerably more productive.

We are shifting away from these distractions, which are low vibrational ploys of the Ego to keep our vibration in the 3D range. Remember, our Ego is our friend. We created it, and its job is to keep our vibration in the 3D range so that we will stay here long enough to have every experience that the Third Density has to offer. As we move towards enlightenment, we can say goodbye and thank you to our Ego. For most of us, it has served us very well indeed.

Although there is still fighting and polluting in many parts of the world, overall, crime statistics are down, philanthropy is up and the world is becoming more sensitized to a higher order of living. This transition is well underway and those with a higher vibration are seeing it more clearly, while those with lower vibrations will likely need a few more lifetimes before they see it at all.

To clarify a point: Those individuals who become enlightened and move to the Fourth Density will still be on Planet Earth, walking amongst us. Their lives, however, will be much easier. Manifestation will be quicker, love and peace will abound for them and everyone will feel much more connected to each other and to The Creator. If we go back to our analogy of the room, for them, the lights will be fully on and they will see everything in the room.

A special thank you to Ricardo Martinez for his teachings on the Shift and on the Ego.

Summary, Part One

- The Creator is everything and everyone. Nothing and no one is outside of or separate from it. All is one; one is all.

- We are included in The Creator. We are light energy beings with all the power and information of the whole.

- We are here in this reality to learn experientially about limitation and separation.

- We created this universe of time, space, duality and matter to have this experience.

- We are spirits, in a physical body, having a human experience.

- To have this experience fully and to play the game fairly, we have to forget what we really are, and we do this each time we are born into a new life.

- Everything and everyone is composed of vibrating, light energy.

- Everything and everyone's energy has its own unique rate of vibration (frequency).

- Vibration correlates with the illusion of solidity or density. Slower vibrations give us the illusion of more density and physicality. Faster vibrations give us the illusion of less physicality and thus, more Spirituality.

- The faster the vibration, the greater the consciousness.

- Vibration has been categorized so that we have seven ranges that we call Densities. These are sometimes referred to as Dimensions of Consciousness.

- Most human vibration falls into a range, that we call the Third Density (3D).

- Some humans, with exceptionally high vibrations, fall into a range that we refer to as the Fourth Density (4D). We call these folks Enlightened.

- Humans are going through a period of acceleration in their evolution, which was centered around "The Shift" of December 21st, 2012.

- This shift in consciousness is being felt more by those with a higher vibration.

- Evidence of this shift is showing up in our various statistics, institutions and earth systems. We designed these systems to keep us in the Third Density for a very long time so that we would have all of the experiences that this density can provide.

- We also created our Ego, a false identity, for the same reason.

- Planet Earth is a sentient being and it is also moving to the Fourth Density.
- Those in 4D will be living side-by-side with those in 3D, on Planet Earth.
- Those with a 4D level of consciousness will be experiencing a more love-based world with a stronger sense of connectedness, physical well being and overall peace.
- Low vibrations correlate with solidity, density and physicality while higher vibrations move us away from these states and advance us towards our natural, spiritual state.

Conclusion, Part One

By nature, we are spirits (souls), inhabiting a physical body in order to have a human experience. As we complete that experience, and all the learning associated with it, we increase our energy vibration, expand our consciousness, and become less physical and more spiritual. The name of the game is to raise vibration.

Against that background, you're possibly wondering: How do I raise my vibration and become more spiritual. That's the subject of Part Two, so read on…

Pursuing Spirituality

IS IT NECESSARY TO PURSUE SPIRITUALITY?

No, not at all. However, we are in this physical realm to have certain experiences. Once we have them, what's the point in hanging around to repeat them? It's like hanging around grade three well after we have learned everything grade three has to offer. We can do it if we want to, but ultimately, we will get bored with grade three and want to move on to richer and more complex experiences.

As well, we are wired to be learning animals. By our nature, we are always learning and seeking new learning experiences. Repeating the same old ones over and over just isn't in our makeup.

Finally, life in the Fourth Density is a lot easier. There is no pain, we have perfect health, love abounds and we can manifest what we want a lot quicker. Most of us are working quite hard for a life like this. Given the chance, why wouldn't we grab it?

So, if we want, we can hang around for a few more lifetimes but sooner or later, with a vibration at the high end of the Third Density, we will wake up and find we are antsy to move on.

HOW SPIRITUAL AM I NOW?

This isn't something that can be easily measured and I certainly don't know how to do it. What this question really comes down to is: What is my vibration now?

Electroencephalographs (EEG) will tell us the vibration rate of the brain. Electrocardiographs (ECG) will do the same for the heart. There are other machines that will measure electrical activity for other organs, and Raman Spectroscopy and Infrared Absorption Spectroscopy will measure the vibration of substances, e.g. water.

Getting a fix on a whole human body is another matter and science, to my knowledge, hasn't come up with an easy solution. I've heard a couple claims of such instruments that purport to do this but I'm not aware of what they are.

Two methods that are common, however, for getting a reading on one's personal vibration are Applied Kinesiology and Dowsing.

Applied Kinesiology, or muscle testing, is fast, accurate and costs next to nothing. The American Chiropractic Association attests to this and reports that Applied Kinesiology is one of the 15 most used chiropractic techniques in the United States, with over 40% of Chiropractors using this technique.

David Hawkins, M.D., PhD, in his best-selling book, Power vs. Force, used muscle testing extensively to design his famous Map of Consciousness, showing human vibratory rates ranging from zero to 1,000 Hertz (beats per second).

Muscle testing can be done in a variety of ways. Usually it is done with one or two people. Here's one way two people can do it. Let's call one person the Operator and the other the Client. The Client would extend his/her arm outward so that it is parallel to the ground. The Operator would ask the Client (whose name is Mary) to make an obviously true statement such as: "My name is Mary". Immediately, the Operator would say to Mary: "Resist" and would then push down on Mary's wrist. Both parties would make note of the amount of pressure needed to push Mary's arm down.

Next, the Operator would ask Mary to say something that is obviously not true, such as: "My name is George". The Operator would immediately again say to Mary: "Resist" and push down on her arm. If Mary is a good subject for muscle testing, her arm will go down with much less effort. Both parties should notice that Mary's arm is significantly better able to resist the Operator's downward pressure when a true statement is made. In other words, the body is stronger in the presence of truth.

Muscle testing can be used in a wide variety of situations. For example, if you wanted to test whether or not a substance is beneficial to eat, you could hold the substance in one hand (some hold it over the heart) and extend the other arm for someone to press downward, using the same "Resist" method as described previously.

I know from personal experience, if you held refined sugar, in your hand or even in your mind, you would test weak. If you held a recently picked apple, most people would test strong. Of course, if you had an allergy to apples, you would be the exception and test weak.

This can also be done by oneself. You could, for example, take the ring finger of one hand and press the tip of it against the tip of the thumb of the same hand, forming a circle. You would then take a finger or thumb (I prefer thumb) on your other hand and insert it into the circle.

After making a statement or holding a substance that you wish to test, press and hold the circle and then pull your inserted finger/thumb through the circle breaking it. If it breaks easily, the statement or substance tested weak. If it took a stronger effort to break the circle, it tested strong. It might take you a few trials before you have a feel for what is a strong result and what is a weak one.

If you are using the ring finger–thumb method with another person as the Operator, you would say to the Client: "Press and Hold" immediately after the statement, and then pull your finger or thumb through the circle.

Another variation is to place your middle or second finger over top of your index finger and push down against the resistance of your index finger. This is probably a more discrete way of testing products in the supermarket.

Muscle testing or Kinesiology, when used consistently with an individual is quite accurate for most people but there is a small percentage where it's not very reliable.

Hawkins points out that when testing a statement, that statement must be clearly stated, with no ambiguity. It must also be a statement related to an existing or past condition or event. According to Hawkins, questions about the future will not elicit reliable results. Some Psychics will disagree but they may have something else operating.

As to measuring an individual's vibration, David Hawkins would take an individual for whom he had previously proven muscle testing to be reliable. He would then proceed to ask that person a series of questions designed to converge on their personal vibration, at that point in time.

For example, he would take such an individual and ask if their vibration was over 150 Hz, if it tested strong, he would then ask if it was over 250. If that question tested strong, he would up the question until it tested weak. Once it tested weak, he had a range for that person; let's say it was strong at 300 but weak at 350. Hawkins might then ask if it was above 325. If it tested strong, he knew it was between 325 and 350; if it tested weak, it was between 300 and 325. He would keep doing this until he converged on a single number.

That's a pretty lengthy and tedious process but that's what he and a number of his fellow researchers did for almost 30 years and their results were then parlayed into a worldwide best seller.

A final note on Hawkins's discoveries: He used a scale of 1–1,000 to calibrate human consciousness. He stated that 1–600 represented the range of consciousness where the vast majority of people reside; 600–1,000 is the realm of extraordinary individuals, sages, mystics, enlightened individuals, etc. He also stated that 204 was a crossover point where readings below 204 indicated something detrimental to the life and evolution of both individuals and society. Readings above 204 indicated the presence of something that was positive and contributory to human evolution and well-being. Another way he stated this was that 204 was the crossover point for integrity — above 204 was truth; below it, was falsehood.

Dowsing is a simpler way to calibrate your own vibration and here I suggest the use of a pendulum. You can use a wide variety of items to make a pendulum. Some can be purchased, already made, or you can use a piece of jewelry or just about anything that will swing with a little weight (called a bob) at the end of a chain, a string or a piece of thread.

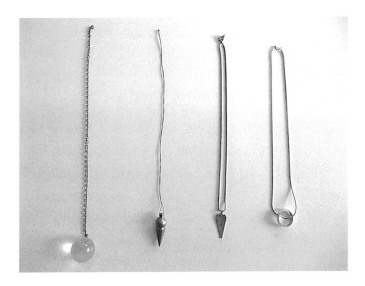

The Photo above shows two store-bought pendulums, on the left, and two that have been improvised — one from a pendant and one from a ring. They will all do the job.

Conventional wisdom says that the thread/chain should be four to six inches from your finger tips to the top of the bob. This can depend on the weight of your bob, as heavier ones often feel better on longer chains (six to eight inches) and lighter ones might be quite comfortable at a couple of inches. The key thing is to test various lengths, see how they perform and then select the length that feels right for you.

There are several ways to use a pendulum. Here is a popular and effective way: Grip your pendulum at the end of the chain or thread that is opposite to the bob. Grip it gently between your forefinger and thumb, and wind any excess thread around your other fingers or keep it in your palm. It is important to ensure that any excess thread doesn't get tangled around the pendulum.

To begin, place the chart or the Yes–No indicator that you intend to use on a table. Sit at the table on a comfortable chair and suspend the pendulum about a half inch above the intersection or focal point of the chart. Anchor the pendulum above the chart by placing your elbow on the table to steady your hand. Start with the pendulum holding still, over the starting point, let your mind go blank and ask a very clear and unambiguous question. The following picture, featuring Fatima Hosseinkhani's elegant right hand (Thank you Fatima), shows how you would begin.

Once the pendulum starts swinging, it is important to let it settle into a final swing. Often, it will start out swinging in one direction, and after a minute or so, will change direction and settle into a stronger and wider swing. The final arc of the swing can sometimes end up being about half the length of the thread. The following picture illustrates a typical, final arc.

Now that you know how and where to hold a pendulum, let's discuss when you might use one. You can use a pendulum to give you a Yes–No or a True–False answer to nearly any declarative statement that refers to the past or present. I haven't been able to make it work for the future any better than chance. I actually put this to the test trying to pick stocks on the Toronto Stock Exchange for a period of about six months. I could have flipped coins for the same results.

The first thing you have to do is figure out which way the pendulum will swing if you are getting a Yes and which way it will swing to indicate a No. Here's how you can do it: Hold your pendulum in place and ask it to give you a Yes. Give it about three or four minutes and see which way it ends up swinging. Let's say it swings vertically, away from you. Ask it for a No, and chances are that it will swing at 90 degrees from Yes or horizontally, side to side. What you might end up with is a pattern like this:

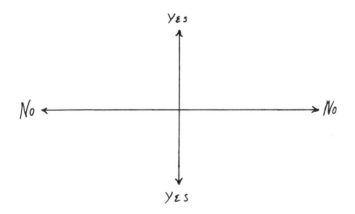

Now, with any Yes–No question that you might have, you can dangle your pendulum in front of you, or if you wish, over the intersection of a chart like the one above. Ask your question and see which way the pendulum swings. You might start with questions for which you know the answers and check that your pendulum is behaving reliably.

Incidentally, you can also do this using your body as a pendulum. You can do this by standing straight and asking yourself for a Yes. Relax and let your body begin to fall whichever way it wishes. Note the direction. For example, it could be forward. Then ask for a No and see which way you body want to move. Chances are, in this example of a Yes being forward, No will be backwards or to one side. Play with this for a while and see if it works for you.

Now that you understand how to use a pendulum, you can begin to use one to gauge your personal vibration. You can do this by devising a chart with the numbers ranging from Zero to whatever number you wish. I suggest you start with one that goes from 0–1,000. This is consistent with ones used by David Hawkins, Stephen Pollitt, Ricardo Martinez and others. The following chart illustrates my point and includes the question that you would either say out loud or hold in your mind.

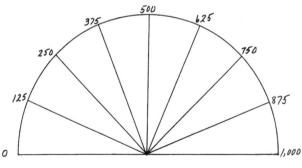

What is My Vibration Now?

If you place your pendulum a half inch or so above the base line, at the intersection of all the spokes, that's your starting point. Ask the question: "What is my vibration now?" and note where the swing ends up. I often ask this question a second time, just as the pendulum starts to move.

It is important to understand that you don't have to have a precise answer, down to a single digit. What's more important is to chart your progress over time. For example, if you are getting a reading of approximately 600 and last month it was more like 500, then you can see that you are progressing.

Two additional points that I think are also important to understand is that, throughout the day, our vibration fluxuates. For example, if you are enjoying a romantic moment with a loved one, chances are your vibration is up. If you just received news that someone close to you was diagnosed with a fatal disease, chances are your vibration will drop. The point here is that a person's vibration is osculating and you would likely get a more valid trend in your vibration if you tested it at the same time each day, e.g. upon rising or just before going to bed.

Another point worth considering is that as the human species is evolving, some of these scales and the points on them may also be evolving. For example, Hawkins says that the majority of people are in the 1–600 range and that approximately half the people on the planet are below 200, with the other half above 200. This was based on his findings through the 1970s to the 1990s. I suggest that, today, given the recent shift in consciousness, he would find that range has moved upward and that 200 is no longer the integrity median for the human species.

A final point is that, to my knowledge, most, if not all, of these researchers are saying that these are not absolute numbers, accurately portraying vibration, in exact Hertz (beats per second). Ricardo Martinez says clearly that the scale he uses employs relative numbers. What I believe he means is that, if near the bottom of the human range of consciousness, we have people operating at around 50 Hz, then enlightened (4D people) are probably somewhere around 800–1000, on a relative scale. Hawkins complicates things considerably more for the lay reader by stating that his "numbers represent the logarithm (to the base 10) of the power of the respective fields," which I don't understand nor feel there is any need to.

My point in all of this is that these numbers are not absolute but are relative. And, they are not very indicative of one's true rate of vibration expressed in Hertz. The important thing is they can be useful for plotting progress and seeing how our vibration is trending.

If you were to use the previous chart and find that you are getting readings towards the high end, you might want to get a new chart with higher calibrations. The one below is an example.

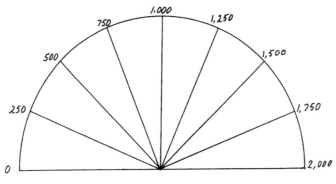

What is My Vibration Now?

After exhausting this chart, you can use the blank one below to calibrate your next one, although, by then, you are probably well on your way to Enlightenment.

Feel free to make your own charts. They don't have to be all that accurate or pretty, and if you find it easier, don't hesitate to photocopy the one below. If you want, you can scan it and blow it up to a larger size or you can put it into a Word document and resize it as you wish. Enjoy...

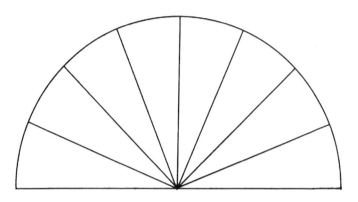

What is My Vibration Now?

Other ways of determining one's approximate vibration is to look at some of the charts that have been developed. Certainly the Hawkins's Map of Consciousness is the most well-known. It is designed as a matrix, with labels for each of the columns. If you scan the chart and find the labels, traits, etc. that apply to you, you can read off the number representing your current vibration. For example, if your God-View is Enabling, your Life-View is Satisfactory, Your Emotion Trust and your process are Release, then you calibrate at 250 and are at a level described as Neutrality.

Other charts, not as well known are The Omega Ultimate Consciousness Chart, The Densities Chart by Nuno Desa, The Oracle Institute's Spectrum of Conscious and Ricardo Martinez's Dimensional Vibro-meter.

Of all the charts I have seen, including Hawkins's, I prefer the Dimensional Vibro-meter because it describes levels of consciousness and quite a few descriptors for each of them. It identifies five levels of consciousness. They are: 3D Low – Asleep, 3D Mid – Aware, 3D High – Awakened, 4D – Enlightened and 5D – Ascended. For each of these levels, we get a description of the individual's spiritual stage, human response, emotional state, love-fear balance and vibration rate, expressed as a range of relative frequencies.

The Vibro-meter also has a rather neat trade-off panel that shows how increases in consciousness correlate with more love and less fear. It also identifies who we connect with at different levels of consciousness, e.g. at the Low 3D level, we are connected to our Ego, whereas at the High 3D level it is the soul and in the fourth dimension, it is with the Higher-Self.

The Dimensional Vibro-meter and its convenient companion chart for using a pendulum can be seen on Ricardo's Spiritual Staircase website at: http://www.spiritual staircase.com/store/c1/Productos_presentados.html.

By now, you're probably wondering: Is he ever going to tell me how I can raise my vibration? Well, here's where we get into it and I'm going to present it in two parts: 1) What is holding it down and 2) How can I raise it?

WHAT IS HOLDING MY VIBRATION DOWN?

A. Subconscious Blockages

Researchers explain that the human mind is split into that part of which we are aware (the conscious mind) and that part of which we are unaware (the subconscious mind). They say that the conscious part of the mind accounts for about 5% of our mental capacity and awareness, and for many people, it could be even less.

Our subconscious mind runs many of the bodily functions that we couldn't possibly keep track of, such as the release of hormones, activating the immune system, regulating blood flow, etc. It also is where we store many of our memories.

It stores at least two kinds of memories: 1) Those from our current life that the mind chooses to repress, or push below our conscious ability to recall. This is a safety measure, so that we are not shocked and overwhelmed by their magnitude, e.g. abuse, criminality, heavy trauma, etc. and 2) Those that come from previous lives. The result of this is that the great majority of us are carrying around a ton of shocking memories that are buried deeply in our subconscious mind and are weighing our vibration down.

Over the course of hundreds of lifetimes, we have experienced a great deal of what the Third Density has to offer.

That includes being bad guys as well as good guys. So if you think about these life times, we have been both victims and perpetrators.

As victims, it would be reasonable that we picked up a lot of baggage that we might label as anger, resentment, suspicion, etc. As perpetrators, we have probably developed such feelings as guilt, unworthiness, inadequacy, etc. What do you think this baggage is doing to our vibration? Of course, it is lowering vibration and most of us are in this situation to some degree.

B. Limiting Beliefs

A belief is the acceptance that a statement is true or that something is real. It has also been described as a thought that we repeat over and over. It seems also that beliefs can be formed in the absence of proof or in the presence of faith.

Beliefs can come from any number of sources. For example, the constant criticism from a misguided parent or teacher can lead a child to believe he is not good enough. A divorce can prompt a child to believe that she is responsible for it. A rape in a past life can lead a woman to believe she is better off being unattractive in this life. Beliefs can come from nearly anywhere, they can be pretty bizarre and they can have a great influence on how we think and behave.

Some beliefs are very empowering, e.g. I believe I can always earn enough money, I believe I am strong and healthy. On the other hand, some beliefs can sap our energy and limit our effectiveness, abundance or happiness, e.g. I'm not worthy, I'm not capable, I should expect to be sick at my age, etc. What do you suppose some of these limiting beliefs do to one's vibration?

C. Stress

Stress isn't caused by an event or a set of circumstances; it's a condition that results from the way we react to events and circumstances. How we react is what gives us stress. For example, two people caught in the same traffic jam might react to it quite differently. One might get agitated and experience rising blood pressure, while the other chills out and listens to music on the radio.

When we react to a situation in a stressful way, like the first driver in the traffic jam, things tighten up, chemicals begin to flow, hormones kick in and we can experience all the wonders of the fight-flight response. This response served us well when it was appropriate to fight or run, but in today's world, fighting and running isn't so convenient. As a result, many of these chemicals are not blown off and they sit and pool in our systems, clogging arteries and generally wearing down our bodies. As our bodies are compromised, so are our minds and we can find ourselves in a downward spiral that can lead to physical or mental disease. When this happens, can you imagine the affect on one's vibration?

Even where the stress isn't so serious, such as the traffic jam, vibration is affected.

D. *Other influences*

In Part One of this book, I wrote about the Ego and pointed out that its job is to keep us in the Third Density until we experience all that this density has to offer. It does this through its many ploys such as always having to be right, having to understand everything, focusing on what's wrong, dwelling on the past, worrying about the future and looking for answers outside of ourselves rather than looking within. These ploys are ingenious and ambush nearly all of us, at one time or another, again, lowering vibration.

Accumulating and clinging to physical possessions can lower vibration. Feng Shui tells us that it can restrict the flow of energy and clutter seems to be a general downer for just about everybody.

Criticism and judgement are big ones. Remember, we are the creators of our reality, so if we criticise something that we don't like, who are we criticising? The key here is to realize that, when we criticise or judge something, we are lowering our vibration to the level of that which we are criticising.

If we look at all of the many conventions, systems and institutions that we have created for this Third Density, we can see how we have created them to hold our vibration in the 3D range. For example, the pharmaceutical industry has a vested interest in keeping us sick, the banks profit when we are in debt, most religions want us to believe we are flawed and should fear God. The food industry emphasizes taste and convenience, producing foods that damage our bodies, our drinking water contains harmful substances and corporations pay the media huge amounts to persuade us to keep in fashion, buy the latest gadget and acquire things we don't need. What do you think all of these conventions, systems and institutions do to our vibration?

Don't get me wrong...these conventions, systems and institutions are not evil. We created them for the purpose of giving ourselves this Third Density experience and they are doing this very effectively. Now, we are starting to awaken and we can begin to see ways to use them that will no longer compromise our vibration.

In concluding this section, it's fair to say that anything we think about or do that either violates another, is fear-based or makes us feel bad will lower vibration.

HOW CAN I RAISE MY VIBRATION?

A. *Hypnosis*

When it comes to clearing blockages that reside deeply in our subconscious mind, Hypnosis can employ three different techniques: Age regression, Past Life Regression and Ego strengthening.

With Age Regression, the client is put into a hypnotic state, and through different techniques, can be taken back in time, to an earlier age when the event happened that caused the blockage. If the blockage was caused by a series of events, removal usually starts by taking the client back to the first event in the series. This first event is referred to as The Initial Sensitizing Event (ISE). Usually, any blockages that exist are due to events that happened before age six and the client has no recollection of them.

Once the ISE is identified, the Hypnotist has several approaches at her disposal, and what she does, depends largely on the severity of the ISE, the number of episodes involved and how disposed the client is to achieving a resolution. An ISE can range from an off-hand remark by a well-intending adult to a long series of abusive attacks.

A case that illustrates the lighter end of this range involved a 40-year old woman who reported that she had no initiative, didn't see projects through to completion and just felt stuck. In hypnosis, she was regressed back to about age five, where she was in a classroom with her Teacher and her classmates. The Teacher said something a bit critical (the ISE) and the little girl interpreted the statement to mean she wasn't good enough.

The Hypnotist asked the 40-year old woman, while still in trance, if there could be other interpretations of that statement. The woman, with some prompting from the Hypnotist, agreed that the Teacher might have been having a bad day, she might have been upset with some of the other children or she might have even had a fight with her husband. The woman agreed, that the belief, "I'm not good enough" was not a reasonable interpretation.

As is usual, once the ISE is discovered and deemed not appropriate, there is some letting go exercise involved. In this case, the Hypnotist asked the client that, if under the circumstances, she could now let that feeling of "I'm not good enough" go. With some gentle prompting, the client indicated that she had let it go.

The Hypnotist then led the client, still in hypnosis, through a forgiving exercise, forgiving the Teacher for inadvertently upsetting the little girl, and herself, for carrying that misinterpretation with her for all those years. Once done, the problem was solved.

Now, let's say a client's problem (excessive anger) is the result of a long series of childhood assaults, perpetrated over a few years. This time, in hypnosis, each sensitizing event (assault) has to be identified and cleared, ideally with as much forgiveness as possible. Although it's a little more complicated, what I'm getting at here is that Age Regression in hypnosis, in certain instances, can be very effective in clearing blockages.

Past Life Regression can work in similar ways. Brian Weiss, MD, is a Psychiatrist who uses hypnosis as one of his therapies. He started out with the belief that there was no such thing as past lives. After numerous patients reported being in Ancient Rome, Medieval Europe and elsewhere in history, he became a believer and produced a number of books on the subject of other lifetimes.

One of Dr. Weiss's books cites the case of a patient who was terribly obese. She tried everything to lose weight and nothing had any effect. In hypnosis, she reported that she was a very beautiful woman, some time ago in a past life. She said, in that life, she was captured, in a war, by enemy soldiers. She was badly abused and vowed that she would never be beautiful again. When she understood that that past life had no bearing on her present life and that her past vow to never be beautiful again was preventing her from losing weight, the pounds began dropping off shortly after the hypnosis session.

When an individual is in hypnosis, he is more receptive and more responsive to suggestion. In cases where Age Regression and Past Life Regression are not yielding any results, the hypnotist can still direct positive suggestions to the subconscious mind, and if the client feels the suggestions are in his best interest, he will likely accept them.

To illustrate, if a client feels that she is not deserving of a good relationship, the hypnotist can make a number of suggestions to the contrary, and if said frequently enough and convincingly enough, the client will begin to accept them, believe them and act accordingly.

Related to this is Self-Hypnosis, where an individual can lay in the suggestions herself — in a sense, self-programming. I'll say more about this in the next section on Meditation.

To sum up, hypnosis can remove blockages, thus raising vibration, through Age Regression, Past Life Regression and positive suggestions made either by the Hypnotist or by oneself. There are other helpful hypnosis techniques but these are three of the more popular ones

B. Meditation

In many respects meditation and hypnosis are the same. There are at least five areas of similarity. In both:

    1. The body becomes very relaxed.

2. Brain waves change from Beta waves to Alpha waves.

3. Metabolism drops significantly.

4. The senses become a little more acute.

5. The subconscious mind comes to the fore, and the client becomes more receptive and more responsive to suggestion.

The major differences are that, in hypnosis, there is a Hypnotist who is directing the agenda. The Hypnotist is operating with her conscious mind and left brain hemisphere, which is analytical, can evaluate and make quick decisions. In meditation, there is only the individual whose subconscious mind and right brain hemisphere is more active. The subconscious mind is a little dozy, not particularly pro-active and happy to sit back and enjoy the peaceful state. In most cases, you could say that meditation is more passive while hypnosis is more active. As well, hypnosis usually has a problem-solving agenda, whereas meditation may not have any agenda at all.

Meditation can raise vibration in at least two ways. First, if we just enjoy it passively, it will calm us down and raise our vibration. Second, while in a state of meditation, we can employ affirmations and visualizations that help us to make positive changes. Before getting into this, I want to present a little background about meditation.

Meditation is not a life style; it is not about religion, philosophy or contemplation. You don't have to wear sandals, sit in contorted positions or make strange sounds.

The practice of meditation has been around for millennia. Although it has been a part of yoga and certain religions for centuries, it wasn't until the late 1950's, that Maharishi Mahesh Yogi introduced Transcendental Meditation to the West. With people like The Beatles, Hans Selye, Deepak Chopra, Clint Eastwood, Joe Namath and California Governor Gerry Brown embracing it, Meditation began to take root in our part of the world. Shortly afterwards, Dr. Herbert Benson of Harvard did much to "legitimize" meditation when he published the results of his research in his popular book, *The Relaxation Response*.

The term meditation is often extended to include pleasant thoughts or themes that can be contemplated. For example, you hear of "Meditations for Teachers," Meditations for Reducing Stress," etc. These can be pleasant and productive ideas to contemplate or mentally dwell upon but they are not meditation. At best, they may be ideas that can be entertained in a state of meditation but they are not, in themselves, meditation.

For our purposes, meditation can be defined as a simple, natural and effortless process for achieving a state of deep relaxation while the mind remains alert and aware. It is a response of the nervous system, where the above-mentioned five changes kick in. It is something that is very peaceful and enjoyable to do.

In sleep, we can also achieve a state of relaxation but our mind is not conscious and we are not aware. As well, we may not be all that relaxed — especially if we are being chased in our dreams by monsters or demons.

Regular meditators find numerous benefits, which have also been demonstrated in laboratory research. Among them are: increases in academic and athletic performance, cardiovascular efficiency, creativity, emotional stability, energy level, interpersonal relations, job performance, learning ability, metabolic stability, nervous system efficiency, perceptual ability, resistance to disease, self-esteem and sociability.

Regular meditators also report decreases in the use of alcohol, cigarettes and non-prescription drugs, as well as decreases in excessive weight, heart rate, high blood pressure, anxiety and depression.

Meditation produces benefits for nearly everyone. On an individual basis, adults, teenagers and children can benefit from it. On a group basis, it is ideal for work groups, social groups, executive committees, clubs and anyone who is interested in improving their competence, happiness and quality of life. It is said, in summary, meditators look younger, are healthier, handle stress better and enjoy life more.

Meditating is easy. Finding the time to meditate, on a regular basis, is the hard part. Most meditators find a regular time and most find the morning, before they start their day, to be best. There is also a fair number who meditate just before their evening meal and some who like to meditate in the evening just before bedtime.

When to meditate is very individual and I recommend that you experiment, taking into account your daily schedule and how meditation affects you. For example, some people prefer to meditate just before bedtime as it helps them to sleep better while others find that meditating in the evening energizes them and makes sleeping difficult.

To induce the meditative response in the nervous system, we need to place our attention on a single action or object so that our mind begins to still itself and stop jumping around from thought to thought. The idea here is that the mind cannot be on more than one thing at a time. It is very quick at bouncing back and forth between ideas, but at any instant, it can only be on one thing.

To place our mind on a singular thing we select what is known as a mantra. A mantra can be a word, a sound, or an object. It might be musical notes, a symbol, one's breathing, someone's voice, a setting sun or a candle flame.

What mantra works best? This is very subjective and I suggest that you experiment until you find one or two that you prefer. I also suggest, when starting out, you use a mantra that involves closing your eyes so as to avoid visual distractions.

Focusing on one's breath seems to work well for many beginners. When doing this, add a couple of words that sync with each inhalation and each exhalation. For example, you could use: in and out, one and two, let and go, etc. When using such words, don't say them out loud, don't whisper them, just think them.

An important point to remember is that the mind cannot be totally controlled. At best, it can be tamed. What typically happens in meditation is that we focus on our mantra and, after a few moments, the mind wanders from the mantra to some distracting thought or idea. This is normal and it is important to relax and realize that this is normal and not "beat oneself up" over it. Just simply and gently come back to the mantra. When the mind wanders again, once again, just bring it back to the mantra and carry on. Pretty soon, perhaps, after five minutes or so, the meditation response will kick in and you will be meditating.

To give it a try, here is a simple procedure:

- Select a quiet environment where you know you won't be disturbed. Disconnect telephones and advise others that you wish to be undisturbed for the next 20 minutes or so.

- Sit on a firm chair, in a comfortable position, back straight, feet flat on the floor, hands in lap, eyes closed.

- Assume a passive attitude — empty the mind of all thoughts and distractions.

- Select a mantra and focus on it. When you notice that your mind has wandered to a thought, just gently come back to your mantra.

- Continue until you wish to stop. Fifteen to twenty minutes is enough for many people but sometimes it is attractive to stay in meditation longer. Don't force anything, just be comfortable.

- When you've had enough or time has run out, open your eyes slowly.

Following are a few additional points to help you meditate more effectively:

- Some people prefer to sit on the floor; others prefer to lie down. Both are fine but each carries a risk. When sitting on the floor, it is important to ensure that the spinal column is straight. When lying down, there is some risk of falling asleep. This isn't a bad thing but it's not meditation.

- If you raise your eyes about 10 degrees, while they are closed, you can induce the meditative state a little more easily.

- It is important that you are not disturbed or that noises such as a ringing telephone or a slamming door don't occur during meditation. You will soon notice that, in the meditative state, your senses are slightly heightened and you will hear things more acutely. When an unexpected noise occurs, you will find it somewhat startling or jarring.

- During meditation, all bodily processes slow down, including digestion. For this reason, it is a good idea to let a couple of hours go by after eating, before meditating. There's no serious downside to this but it can be a little uncomfortable and distracting to have a lump of food sitting in the digestive track.

- The amount of light in the room while meditating is a matter of individual preference. Experiment until you find the level of lighting you prefer. Most people prefer some reduction from normal daylight but the preferences do span a wide range.

- Soft, upholstered chairs can sometimes be too soft and not provide the proper amount of support to maintain a straight spinal column. Often the best chairs are straight backed and fairly firm in the seat.

- For the first few times, when sitting up straight, you may find your head tending to fall forward or backward. By adjusting your body forward or backward, you will come to a balance point where this soon becomes a non-issue.

- While in meditation, with eyes closed, it is common to see visuals. These can range from vivid objects and scenes to simple colours. This is normal and usually quite pleasant. Don't be alarmed, just enjoy the experience.

- Sometimes, especially when a little sleep-deprived, we relax so much that our brain wave activity falls to Theta, four to eight beats per second. Theta is the brain wave activity that accompanies dreaming. It can happen, that while you are meditating, a little dream scenario will flit by. Again, relax; this is normal and fairly common. If this does happen, you will notice, that much like dreaming in sleep, we can quickly lose the ability to recall these meditation dreams.

The old brainwashing techniques of the 1950's taught us that if you say something often enough, you will eventually come to believe it. And, when we believe something to be true, the subconscious mind will find a way to make it true.

The subconscious mind is not judgemental; it just accepts what it is being told and acts upon it. It is the processor while our conscious mind is the programmer. The thoughts and ideas that the conscious mind chooses to run can be thought of as programs and the subconscious mind is what runs them.

Some scientists have said that we generate thousands of thoughts every day, most of which are negative or worrisome. If the subconscious mind is processing predominately negative thoughts, is it any surprise that the resultant reality is mostly negative?

We can control that. We can choose the thoughts that we run through our conscious mind for the subconscious mind to process. If we choose pleasant, positive thoughts, then the resultant reality will be pleasant and positive. It's our choice.

We all know people who constantly revel in negativity and we see the kind of reality they get. On the other hand, we all know people who are continually upbeat and positive, and they seem to live in a much more positive reality. In effect, they have a higher vibration, their level of consciousness is higher and they experience a more pleasant reality.

If we don't like the reality we are experiencing, we can choose to change the program. One way to change it is to affirm to the subconscious mind statements (affirmations) that are positive and descriptive of what we would like to have in our reality.

Stating affirmations, as though they are already achieved, in a state of meditation enhances their power because, the subconscious mind cannot tell the difference between reality and fantasy. As well, in this state, the subconscious is more receptive and responsive to suggestion.

Here are a few example affirmations:

- I love myself without reservation and always think of myself in a positive light.

- I know that everyone is a part of The Creator and a part of me. For this reason, I love everyone without conditions.

- As everyone is part of The Creator, I look for opportunities to meet and engage with new people. I always find that the more I like and enjoy them, the more they like and enjoy me.

- As long as no one violates anyone, I always allow how others behave and see reality.

- I am completely responsible for all of my thoughts, actions and circumstances.

- I enjoy perfect health. My body is strong, vibrant, flexible and agile. I feel energetic, powerful and I never get sick.

- I always take things in stride and approach life relaxed, confident and self-assured.

- As part of The Creator, my creativity is always expanding and expressing itself in new and interesting ways.

- I have an excellent memory and can recall everything that I have ever learned or experienced.

- I am completely successful at everything I do.

In meditation, affirmations can be handled in a variety of ways:

- You might choose to deal with only a few at a time.

- You could record a few and have them playing while you are meditating.

- You could have someone read them to you, in which case the pronouns would change from I to you.

- Consider using them at other times, e.g. while standing before a mirror, while driving a car or just before sleep, as we fall into an alpha state.

To make affirmations really catch hold, say them in conjunction with visuals. Create a little movie of you already having and enjoying that which you are affirming. If it's a new car you want, see yourself driving it, smell the new car smell, feel the power of the engine, hear the sound of the wind rushing by, get excited and enjoy the new car experience. Employ your senses and your emotions. The subconscious loves movies — the more exciting and sensual, the better.

Final Note: Some people find that listening to an external voice helps them to keep their mind off all the day-to-day chatter and settle more easily into a deep meditative state. There are recordings that provide this experience and one can be found on my website if you copy this address into your browser: http://www.peterhdennis.com/A_Guided_Meditation.php.

C. Activations

I have seen individuals lead a guided meditation, and when everyone is in a deeply mellow state, call upon higher entities to come and clear some of the blockages.

These entities can be Ascended Masters (e.g. St. Germain), Angels or channeled individuals (e.g. Bashar). It is difficult to say exactly what is going on but there is a purported clearing happening. As well, I have seen individuals do this either with their touch (e.g. Srinivas Arka) or by intention (e.g. Ricardo Martinez).

As well, just being in the presence of an exceptionally high vibrational individual can raise the vibration of all around and result in the clearing of many blockages.

D. *Food*

Increasing vibration is a three pronged mission: Body, mind and spirit. In pursuing Spirituality, most of us don't pay much attention to the body, and we focus instead on the mind and the soul.

To address the body, let's first look at how we fuel it. As I stated earlier, everything is composed of energy. As a result, if we eat something, we take in its energy as well as any nutrients that it may contain.

Food's energy comes from the sun and its nutrients come from the soil. Eating living food gives us more energy and carries a higher vibration than eating dead animals or manufactured commodities.

Most educated people, these days, recognize that nutrition is important and many of us are supplementing because we can't easily find the nutrition we need in grocery stores. Even though we may be supplementing and covering our nutritional needs, we may be doing it without improving our vibration. There are foods that are high in nutrition, yet low in vibration, e.g. vitamin pills or protein bars.

The ideal is to find food that is both high in vibration and nutrition. These foods are usually found on trees, plants and growing in the ground. Eating raw food, organically grown food and juicing are ways to get life force energy into our bodies, while a Naturopathic Doctor or nutritionist can round out the picture with supplements.

To avoid lowering our body's vibration with food, it is helpful to realize that we have diverted food's purpose from providing the body with energy to a focus on taste and convenience. Today, we have fast food, super-sized food, genetically modified food, food grown with hormones, antibiotics, steroids, pesticides, insecticides and other chemicals that do harm to the body and lower our overall vibration.

Our bodies are the vehicles in which we live while having this human experience. We can neglect our bodies and still have a human experience, but if our interest is pursuing Spirituality, then high vibrational and nutritious food will further that cause. Falling into the traps of today's modern, harmful and low vibrational foods will compromise it.

E. Water

By weight, more than half the human body is water. It's higher in infants and generally lower as we age. With water being such a large component of our bodies, its quality has a major impact on our state of health, and of course, our state of health has a major influence on our vibration.

North American tap water, approved for drinking, contains added chemicals, and often other contaminates such as arsenic and heavy metals. Chlorine is one of the chemicals, and although it is used to kill off bacteria and viruses, it produces what are known as disinfection by-products. Some of these by-products increase the risk of cancer and have been shown to increase the incidence of miscarriage.

Hydrofluoric acid is another chemical additive. Although it was added to reduce tooth decay, it is also used to refine high octane gasoline, to make chlorofluorocarbons for freezers and air conditioners, and to produce a number of other products such as fluorescent light bulbs, plastics and herbicides. The amounts of hydrofluoric acid in our tap water is not likely to be lethal. It is, however, harmful, e.g. in 2010, a study by The U.S. Center for Disease Control and Prevention determined that 40.7% of adolescents aged 12–15 had dental fluorosis, a serious disease caused by exposure to fluoride. Aside from health risks, advocates for banning fluoride from public drinking water also cite the extra cost, environmental pollution and the violation of human rights.

I won't get into the affects of arsenic or heavy metals on human health; you can look into that yourself. As well, if you check bottled water, you will find that many are no better than tap water.

I think, by now, you get my point: Tap and most bottled water is not high vibrational and many people, in third world countries, don't even get to drink tap water.

We hear that it is important to drink lots of water each day. Experts say the correct amount differs widely depending on factors such as gender, age, eating habits, exercise routines, environmental temperature, state of health, etc. Although there are some finely-engineered formulae for determining the correct amount to consume, overall, the old guideline of eight, eight ounce glasses per day is more or less in the ballpark for most of us, taking into account our consumption of liquid in other forms, e.g. juice, lettuce, watermelon, etc.

The best water we are told is either distilled water or reverse osmosis water. Neither is easily available to most people. The former has to be purchased by the bottle and carted home while the latter involves a rather expensive installation. Nevertheless, if water is such a large component of the body and we are trying to raise our body's vibration, drinking lots of the cleanest water will have a significant impact.

Taking water a step further, we find that it is both unique and interesting. It is a liquid, formed at normal pressure and temperature, when two gasses are combined. It is able to record and carry information from a molecule that is no longer present and it is the necessary medium for molecular signals to be transmitted in the body.

Dr. Masaru Emoto, from Japan, is famous for his research on water in which he froze water and started observing the resultant crystals with a microscope. He observed water from a variety of sources and found that the water coming from pristine areas produced beautiful crystals, whereas he could not get anything as attractive from tap water or from the rivers and lakes near large cities. The most beautiful crystals came from twice-distilled hospital water.

What is really interesting is that Dr. Emoto and his staff began seeing the most beautiful crystals when they repeated what he called: "Good words, good music and pure prayer". Alternatively, when they offered such words to the water as "you stupid water", "I hate you", "You are ugly", they got disfigured, unsightly crystals.

Dr. Emoto also found that he could change the appearance of water crystals, not only by saying a word(s) but by writing a word(s) and placing it in proximity to the water. He then went on to discover that all he had to do was think the word(s) and the water would change.

He concluded from all of this, that at the atomic level, there is a vibrational pattern in all matter (Sound familiar?). This, he believes, is the basis of human consciousness and our thoughts can change a substance's vibration, and thus, the substance itself.

Stephen Pollitt has taken Dr. Emoto's research and applied it to human health. In his book: Heal Thyself, he describes how he has designed and tested various symbols which he has placed in proximity to water. After thousands of tests he has identified symbols which he says structure and then charge the water. He refers to these symbols as Source Energy Medicines (SEM).

Pollitt's research has created well over one hundred different SEMs. He has about 60 different remedies for what he calls Transformation, e.g. T1 – Bacteria Transformation, T2 – Virus Transformation, T9 – Cancer cell Transformation, etc. Pollitt has 28 remedies for Attitude of Allowance, e.g. AA2 – Attitude of Joy, AA5 Attitude of Gratitude, AA7 – Attitude of Compassion, etc. He has others for Balance, e.g. B1 – Balance Polarity, B3 Balance Body PH, BB47 – Balance Sleep, etc. And, he has yet others for Restoration, e.g. R1 – Restoration for males, R9 – Restoration for DNA, R31 – Restoration for the Limbic System, etc.

Pollitt found that if he combined all of the remedies from one category, he had a Fusion Remedy, which was just as effective as taking all of that category's remedies individually. This simplified things considerably and he then developed Fusion Remedies for each of the categories: Transformation, Balance, Attitude Adjustment, Restoration and Energy Level Progression.

The whole idea here is that Pollitt's symbols will change the energetic vibration of the water. If we drink the water, over a prescribed period of time, the water will clear disease, and other blockages so that we can raise our personal vibration.

Pollitt provides his symbols free of charge, on his website and his book tells readers how to use them. I suggest, if you download his symbols and use them, you make an online donation to his research. You can find his website at: http://sourceenergyresearch.net.

F. Aromatherapy

Essential oils are so named, not because they are essential to health, but because they are the essence of a plant's fragrance. They can go by other names, such as Volatile oil, Othereal oil or "Oil of", such as Oil of Oregano.

Essential oils are usually extracted from plants by a distillation process. They are used in soaps, perfumes, cosmetics, household cleaning products and to add flavours to food and drink. Some can be ingested and some are topical.

The scientific research on their efficacy is a bit sketchy but the distillation process can make them highly vibrational. Some involve elaborate processing and can cost over $100 for a 5ml bottle, e.g. Sacred Frankincense. Essential oils are often used to clear blockages, improve mental, emotional and physical health, and raise an individual's vibration.

Flower Essences are similar and have the same intent of clearing blockages, improving health and raising vibration. Many practitioners make their own essences and are quite intuitive when it comes to selecting flowers and recommending essences to their clients.

Interestingly, the magic of water comes into play here: When making an essence, a few flowers of the type selected are floated on water and left in sunlight for at least a couple of hours. The essence of the flowers is imprinted vibrationally on the water. The water retains and carries this vibration while it is mixed in a glass bottle with an equal portion of alcohol. From this solution, a few drops are again mixed with alcohol to become a stock bottle from which the remedies are made.

I know the above descriptions are simplistic and incomplete, and may not be the only way flower essences are produced but my objective in presenting Aromatherapy is to point out that the essential oils and flower essences can play an important role in raising one's vibration. If you are interested in learning more about how they are made, how you can purchase them, how best to choose them and use them, I suggest you speak with one or more of the people who have some real expertise.

G. Acceptance

As we are The Creators, or co-creators of our reality, what we see around us is our creation. As well, what we create is a reflection of who we are and what is going on within us.

With those two ideas in mind, if we are experiencing something that we don't like or is giving us a hard time, these two ideas have the potential to give us considerable relief and raise our vibration.

To illustrate, suppose we have a boss who is constantly criticising our work and we find this to be unfair and stressful. First, if we recognize that this character is our creation or co-creation, we have to acknowledge that we are responsible for his existence. Second, we have to acknowledge that this boss is a reflection of what's going on inside of us — in effect, he represents a message that something inside of us needs to be fixed.

Just the simple acceptance that we are responsible for this situation and that there is a message for us to fix something within ourself goes a long way towards softening the situation and raising vibration.

Then the question becomes: If there is something within us that needs attention, what is it and how do we deal with it? Well, either we know what the solution is (possibly we are too critical?) or we don't. If we know what it is, then we can do something about it. If we don't know what is going on to cause this problem, we can accept it and allow the Higher-Self to deal with it at an appropriate time. Either way, the situation de-escalates and our vibration increases.

H. Thoughts

I mentioned before that scientists have found that most of us entertain thousands of thoughts every day and most of them are negative. As this would lower most people's vibration, how do we get out of this pattern and think more positively?

There are two strategies that have each proven effective. One is to say the word "switch" whenever you find yourself mired in a negative thought(s). When you say this, immediately go to a favourite, pleasant thought, e.g. a loved one, an achievement you feel proud of, an activity you enjoy, etc.

The second strategy comes from Dr. Wayne Dyer. He suggests wearing an elastic band on your wrist and points out that this is best done with a buddy. The idea is that whenever you find yourself thinking negatively, give the elastic a gentle snap and change your thinking, again, to something more high vibrational. Dr. Dyer suggests that your buddy can help by catching you when you express a negative thought aloud. The buddy, however, does not get to snap the elastic.

I. Other Vibration Raisers

Up until now, Part Two has provided a fair bit of detail about how each of the various techniques and therapies work. What follows here are some examples of everyday things we can all do to raise vibration. They may not work for everyone, e.g. dancing could be uncomfortable for some, but overall, they should help most of us, most of the time. Here they are:

- Love everything and everyone, as part of the whole, as much as you can, without conditions.

- Be grateful. An attitude of gratitude is one of the most powerful vibration raisers. A prayer of gratitude is more effective (high vibrational) than a prayer of petition.

- Accept that what we see around us is a reflection of what is inside of us. Accept that we are responsible for the things around us, including the things we don't like. These things that we don't like are messages for which we can be thankful and then take action.

- Practice allowance and acceptance, and reduce or eliminate criticism and judgement. This is a big one, and for me, a life-time pursuit.

- Forgiveness is a huge game-changer. When we are mired in the negativity of harbouring hate, resentment, revenge, etc. our vibration is very low. Forgiving transgressions releases a great deal of that negativity and vibration takes a giant leap upward. Similarly, forgiving ourselves for carrying around all of this low vibrating negativity can be immensely liberating.

- Help others. Many of us seem to be wired to do this. Lately, the media has been reporting some of the world's wealthiest people donating sizeable chunks of their fortunes to charity. Paying it forward can be a real kick while raising our abundance vibration.

- Hang around high vibrational people. When two people are together, usually the one with the higher vibration will raise the other's just by being in their presence.

- Laugh. Norman Cousins, after learning that he had terminal cancer, watched slap-stick comedies and laughed himself back to health.

- Get rid of attachments. It's often amazing how we lighten up when we get rid of clutter and useless stuff. It's better yet if we can give it to someone who can make better use of it.

- Play or listen to uplifting music. There has been considerable research on this subject and I think we intuitively gravitate towards it when we have the opportunity.

This list can go on but I think you get the idea that thinking thoughts and engaging in actions that make us feel good raises our vibration. Just about anything that makes us feel good qualifies, e.g. singing, dancing, loving sex, whatever.

We have a built-in guidance system that serves us well if we pay attention and it's found in our emotions. Although Psychologists can label and identify a multitude of emotions, they all boil down to two kinds: those that make us feel good and those that make us feel bad. If we are doing things that make us feel good, we are on the right track and we are raising our vibration.

J. The Law of Attraction

Although I've pretty much finished this short book, I think it is important to add this law because it depends so much on vibration.

You have probably heard the Law of Attraction expressed in a variety of ways, e.g. "What you put out is what you get back," "We attract what we think about" or "Likes attract likes." Likes attract likes really means that a vibration attracts a similar vibration, and that is the key to making this law manifest what we want.

Quantum Physics is demonstrating that thought does move matter and that by thinking certain thoughts, we get predictable outcomes. For example, if an observer expects a quantum (currently the tiniest observable object) to behave as a particle, it will. If the observer expects the quantum to behave as a wave, that's the way it will behave. In effect, our thoughts direct energy to create our reality and everything in it.

If we spend time thinking about something positive that we want, we can attract it, thus demonstrating the power of positive thinking. If we spend time thinking about something negative that we don't want, we will attract it as well, thus demonstrating the power of negative thinking.

Most of us do not focus our thoughts very well. We think about things we want, things we don't want, things we love, things we fear, and because the Law of Attraction always works perfectly, this collection of conflicting and confused thoughts creates a haphazard and mixed result. When this happens, we are not creating on purpose, we are creating aimlessly. To work the Law of Attraction to our advantage, we need to be very disciplined and laser-like in our thinking.

Managing The Law of Attraction to achieve exactly what we want is tricky. There are a number of things that need to be taken into account. They are:

- We need to be very clear when thinking about or expressing exactly what we want. To focus our thoughts and concentrate them on what we want, it is helpful to write goal statements, in cursive script, describing exactly what we want. One way to do this is make sure that each statement of intent is Specific, Measurable, Attainable, Realistic and Trackable/Time-related (**SMART**). Edit and rewrite them until you are satisfied that you have very tight, clear, **SMART** statements of exactly what you want.

- Once we have clear, concise goal statements, we need to declare that we want them. Some do this in prayer to God, Source, The Universe or some express an intention that the subconscious mind can work on. To me, these are all the same thing, so whatever works best for you is the way to go.

- When expressing our want(s), it adds energy if we visualize. That is, run a little movie in your mind of what it would be like to have the goal. See its attributes and features; feel the enjoyment derived from having it. Employ the senses and the emotions — all of these add potency. As well, visualizing works best when we are in an altered state of consciousness, such as hypnosis, self-hypnosis, meditation, or just before falling asleep.

- In expressing our intention, some say we should state our intention, in an almost obsessive way, repeating it over and over, at every opportunity. Others say: Articulate your goal and then release it, forget about it, and allow the Universe to do its thing. My view is that both work and each can be effective. The key element is belief — if you believe one approach works, it probably will, and it doesn't really matter which one you pick.

- We have to discipline ourselves and focus our thoughts on what we want and be sure not to dwell on the lack of it. For example, if we want peace, then love peace, don't hate war. If we want wellness, think about health and don't dwell on illness or disease. If we want wealth, think about money and abundance and not about upcoming bills or the lack of funds.

- We have to ensure that we are living at a vibrational level that matches the vibration we set up when we first decided on what we wanted. To illustrate, suppose you want a new car. When you think about this car, you get excited and this excitement sets up a vibration that is higher than normal for you. Now, if you are living your life in fear, always thinking negative thoughts, your vibration will not be a match for the vibration you have set up when thinking about the new car. There is mismatch here. When thinking about our goal, our vibration is at one level and when living most of our life, it's at another. Because the two are not on the same level, they can't exist together, likes cannot attract likes and the goal can't be achieved.

- Some people think that expressing our intentions is best stated with the words: "I want..." I disagree because if we declare a want to The Universe, that's exactly what we will get — a want, or more wanting. I think it's better to express such words as: "I have, I am, I enjoy my ..., I love my..., I am grateful for..., etc."

- As a matter of fact, gratitude is one of the highest vibrational thoughts we can have. An attitude of gratitude will go a long way towards raising and keeping our vibration at a level that will attract what we want.

- Many of us harbor limiting beliefs such as: We are not worthy, I don't deserve to have it, it's just not possible, all rich people are crooks, etc. Henry Ford said: "If you believe it is or if you believe it isn't, you're right." Belief, or expectation, is critical to manifesting our goals and developing a new belief or getting rid of an undesirable one is not always easy. As I explained earlier, we often don't even know what our beliefs are, as they can be buried deeply in our subconscious.

- Someone once said: "Failing to plan is planning to fail." A plan is a delineation of the steps (often mini-goals) that we intend to take in order to reach our intended target. If a goal doesn't at least start with a plan, then it's merely a wish and lacks potency. In reality, however, goals are often achieved in ways that the planner never envisaged, and the journey to achieving the goal, with its various twists and turns, is more of a learning experience than ever originally intended.

- Some action on our part is required, even if only a first step. Leaving it all to "The Universe" isn't usually enough. If you want to win the lottery, you have to buy a ticket.

- If a goal conflicts with one of our values, we are setting up a dissonance that will frustrate the goal's achievement. For example, if we want a career as a senior executive and we strongly value family, we probably won't achieve the career, or hold it for long if that position involves long hours and frequent travel. Usually, values trump goals.

- Our goal may not be consistent with our soul's purpose. For example, if we came into this life with the purpose of experiencing poverty, we likely will not experience wealth.

- Finally, we have to remember that we are in the Third Density where we set out to experience something opposite to our true nature. Part of our true nature is that we are unlimited. In coming to this realm, we chose to experience limitation. This density is also bound by time. The combination of these two ideas does not usually support instant manifestation. Instant manifestation is a phenomenon of the Fourth Density, not this one. Occasionally, we hear of instant or nearly-instant manifestations. When we do, I think we are hearing about individuals who either carry a high vibration or have raised it temporarily to a level where time is more malleable, as it is in or near the level of Fourth Density

The Law of Attraction has been written and spoken about for centuries. I have over a dozen sources on my bookshelf. The earliest source I know of is from Plato in the year 391

B.C., "The Law of Affinity." After that, I have "The Master Key", which was published in 1912. This is followed by Napoleon Hill's "Think and Grow Rich," Norman Vincent Peale's "Power of Positive Thinking," Earl Nightingale's "The Strangest Secret," right up to modern day works by Brian Tracy, Ester and Jerry Hicks (Abraham), Deepak Chopra, and Wayne Dyer. They all pretty much say the same thing:

- Get a clear picture of what you want.

- Declare it and choose your words carefully.

- Think about it and not the lack of it.

- Have a plan and take some action.

- Eliminate limiting beliefs, if you can identify them.

- Ensure that your goals are consistent with your values and life purpose.

- Keep your vibration up.

Summary, Part Two

- It is not at all necessary to pursue Spirituality, but sooner or later, we all will.

- Measuring human vibration is not an exact science. Kinesiology and dowsing with a pendulum are quite effective for many people. These won't yield exact numbers but they can be consistent and show you how your vibration is progressing.

- There are some charts that can also lead one to identify an approximate level of consciousness.

- It's ideal to take these measures at the approximate same time of day as our vibration oscillates throughout the day, depending on mood, energy level, etc.

- Some things that most of us are involved with that lower our vibration include:

  - Powerful emotional memories that are buried deeply in our subconscious from events in this life and/or past lives. Events that created anger, sadness, resentment and self-hatred are examples.

  - Limiting beliefs that were created either in this life or in past ones.

- Stressful reactions to life's events.

- Our Ego and its various ploys.

- Many of the world's institutions, systems and conventions, which are fear-based, emphasize survival and condition us to think and behave in ways that are opposite to our true nature.

- Judging and criticising others.

- Hanging on to attachments.

• Strategies and practices that can raise our vibration include:

- Hypnosis, through Age and Past Life Regression can probe the subconscious mind and uncover the sensitizing events that are causing present-day negative emotions and clear them away. It can also reveal limiting beliefs and replace them with more empowering ones.

- The practice of regular meditation can also clear away limiting beliefs and negative emotions. It can do this with added potency if affirmations and visualizations are used.

- Spiritual activations or clearings.

- Eating, clean, organic, high energy food.

- Drinking clean and positively charged (as per Stephen Pollitt) water.

- Aromatherapy with high vibrational essential oils and flower essences.
- Practice love without conditions.
- Turn negative thoughts into positive ones.
- Acceptance that what is around us is a reflection of what is within us.
- Adopt an attitude of gratitude.
- Practice forgiveness.
- Reduce or eliminate judgement and criticism.
- Associate with high vibrational people.
- Laugh.
- Help others.
- Get rid of attachments.
- Play or listen to uplifting music.

• The law of Attraction is a law about vibration. As vibrations attract similar vibrations, the higher we can raise ours, the more we will attract what we want and the faster we will attract it.

Conclusion, Part Two

Advancing towards Spirituality is an exercise in raising our vibration. The more we raise it, the more we are expanding our consciousness. As our consciousness expands, we become less physical, and more spirit-like or Spiritual.

We know we are raising our vibration when we engage in thoughts and actions that make us feel good and give us peace. The bottom line is our state of peace. If what we are doing gives us peace, keep doing it; if it doesn't, do something else that does.

Bibliography

Anka, Darryl. *BASHAR: Blueprint for Change*. SimiValley, CA. New Solutions Publishing.1990.

Arka, Srinivas. *Adventures in Self-Discovery*. London, U.K. Minerva Press. 1998.

Bays, Brandon and Billett, Kevin. Consciousness The New Currency. Cowbridge, United Kingdom. Journey Publications Ltd. 2009.

Benson, Herbert. *The Relaxation Response*. New York, NY. Avon Books. 1975.

Byrne, Rhonda. *The Secret*. Hillsboro, OR. Beyond Words Publishing. 2006.

Chadwick, Gloria. *Discovering Your Past Lives*. Chicago Illinois. Contemporary Books, Inc. 1988.

Davis, Roy Eugene. *An Easy Guide To Meditation*. Lakemont, GA. CSA Press, Publishers. 1988.

Day, Laura. *Practical Intuition*. New York, Broadway Books. 1996.

Denning, Melita and Phillips, Osborne. *The Llewellyn Practical Guide to Astral Projection*. St. Paul, MN. Llewellyn Publications. 1988.

Dyer, Dr. Wayne W. *The Power of Intention*. Carlsbad, CA. Hay House Inc. 2004.

Frissell, Bob. *Nothing in This Book Is True, But It's Exactly How Things Are*. Berkeley, CA. Frog Ltd. 1994.

Graves, Tom. *The Elements of Pendulum Dowsing*. Shaftesbury, Dorset, UK. Element Books Limited. 1989.

Goldberg, Dr. Bruce. *New Age Hypnosis*. Woodbury, MN. Llewellyn Publications. 1998.

Goldsmith, Joel S. *The Art Of Meditation*. New York, NY. Harper and Row, Publishers, Inc. 1956.

Haanel, Charles F. *The Master Key*. Calgary, AB. Prosperity Secrets.com Inc. Originally published 1912. 2002.

Hand Clow, Barbara. *The Pleiadian Agenda*. Santa Fe, NM. Bear & Company, Inc. 1995.

Hanson, Peter G. *The Joy of Stress*. Toronto, ON, Canada. Stoddart Publishing Co. Limited. 1986.

Hawkins, David R. *Power vs. Force*. Sedona, AR. Hay House, Inc. 2002.

Hicks, Ester and Jerry. *Ask and it is Given*. Carlsbad, CA. Hay House Inc. 2004.

Hicks, Ester and Jerry. *The Amazing Power of Delibert Intent*. Carlsbad, CA. Hay House Inc. 2006.

Hill, Napoleon. *Think and Grow Rich*. United States. Ballantine Books. 1937.

Hunter, C. Roy and Eimer, Bruce N. *The Art of Hypnotic Regression Therapy*. Carmarthen, Wales. Crown House Publishing Ltd. 2012.

Institute for Enlightenment. *A Handbook For Humanity*. Portland, OR. Strawberry Hill Press. 1992.

Kason, Yvonne. *A Farther Shore*. Toronto, ON, Canada. HarperCollins. 1994.

Marciniak, Barbara. *Earth, Pleiadian Keys to the Living Library*. Santa Fe, NM. Bear & Company, Inc. 1995.

McWilliams, Peter. *Life 101*. Los Angeles, CA. Prelude Press. 1994.

Moore, Marcia. *Hypersentience*. New York, NY. Bantam Books, Inc. 1976.

Newton, Michael. *Journey of Souls*. Woodbury, MN. Llewellyn Publications. 1994.

Newton, Michael. *Destiny of Souls*. Woodbury, MN. Llewellyn Publications. 2000.

Newton, Michael. *Life Between Lives*. Woodbury, MN. Llewellyn Publications. 2004.

Newton, Michael. *Memories of the Afterlife*. Woodbury, MN. Llewellyn Publications. 1994.

Nightingale, Earl. *The Strangest Secret*. Chicago, IL. Nightingale Conant Corporation. 1986.

Paulson, Genevieve Lewis. *Kundalini and the Chakras*. St. Paul, MN. Llewellyn Publications, Inc. 1993.

Pendleton, Don and Linda. *To Dance With Angels*. New York, NY. Kensington Publishing Corp. 1990.

Pollitt, Stephen Joseph. *Heal Thyself*. Indian Hills, CO. Self-published. 2007.

Ridall, Kathryn. *Channeling, How to Reach Out to Your Spirit Guides*. New York, NY. Bantam Books. 1988.

Roberts, Jane. *The Coming of Seth*. New York, NY. Pocket Books. 1966.

Roberts, Jane. *The Seth Material*. New York, NY. Bantam Books. 1972.

Roberts, Jane. *Seth Speaks*. New York, NY. Bantam Books. 1974.

Roberts, Jane. *The Nature of Personal Reality*. New York, NY. Bantam Books. 1974.

Roberts, Jane. *The Unknown Reality, Volume One*. New York, NY. Bantam Books. 1977.

Roberts, Jane. *The Unknown Reality, Volume Two — Part One*. New York, NY. Bantam Books. 1977.

Roberts, Jane. *The Unknown Reality, Volume Two — Part Two*. New York, NY. Bantam Books. 1977.

Roberts, Jane. *The Nature of The Psyche.* New York, NY. Bantam Books. 1979.

Roman, Sanaya and Packer, Duane. *Opening to Channel.* Tiburon, CA. H J Kramer Inc. 1987.

Royal, Lyssa & Priest, Keith. *The Prism of Lyra.* Phoenix, AZ. Royal Priest Research Press. 1992.

Royal, Lyssa & Priest, Keith. *Visitors from Within.* Phoenix, Arizona. Royal Priest Research Press. 1992.

Sharamon, Shalila and Baginski, Bodo J. *The Chakra Handbook.* Federal Republic of Germany. Lotus Light Publications. 1991.

Sutphen, Dick. *Radical Spirituality.* Malibu, CA. Valley of the Sun Publishing. 1995.

Talbot, Michael. *The Holographic Universe.* New York, NY. Harper Colins Publishers. 1991.

Voigt, Anna. *Simple Meditation for everydat relaxation and rejuvenation.* Vancouver, BC. Raincoast Books. 2001.

Walsch, Neale Donald. *Conversations With God, Book 1.* New York, NY. G.P. Putnam's Sons.1995.

Walsch, Neale Donald. *Conversations With God, Book 2.* New York, NY. G.P. Putnam's Sons. 1997.

Walsch, Neale Donald. *Conversations With God, Book 3.* New York, NY. G.P. Putnam's Sons. 1998.

Webster, Richard. *Spirit Guides & Angel Guardians.* St. Paul, MN. Llewellyn Publications. 1998.

Weiss, Brian L. *Through Time into Healing.* New York, NY. Fireside, Simon and Schuster. 1992.

What the Bleep Do We Know. Beverley Hills, CA. Capture Light & Lord of The Wind Films. 2004

Zukav, Gary. *The Seat Of The Soul.* New York, NY. Fireside. 1989.

HANDWRITING ANALYSIS

An Adventure in Self-Discovery, 3rd Edition

$18.95 in most bookstores

This book explains all you need to know about Handwriting Analysis in order to produce a comprehensive profile of anyone's personality. It provides a sound introduction to the subject, shows you how to identify over 80 different aspects of personality and it gives you everything necessary to produce comprehensive and revealing analyses.

After selling more than 10,000 printed copies, this book has been converted to various electronic versions and sells online for $5.99. It can be purchased from most online retailers, including:

- Chapters/Indigo: http://www.chapters.indigo.ca
- Amazon.ca: http://www.amazon.ca
- Amazon.com: http://www.amazon.com
- Barnes & Nobel: http://www.barnesandnoble.com
- The Apple Store: https://itunes.apple.com
- Kobo: http://store.kobobooks.com

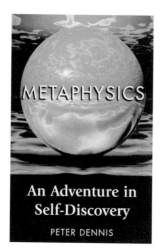